IT'S KIDSTUFF

by

ROGER

ITV Books/Arrow Books

Jointly published by

INDEPENDENT TELEVISION BOOKS LTD
247 Tottenham Court Road,
London W1P 0AU

and

ARROW BOOKS LTD
3 Fitzroy Square,
London W1

An imprint of the Hutchinson Publishing Group

London Melbourne Sydney Auckland
Wellington Johnannesburg and agencies
throughout the world

First published 1981
Reprinted 1981
© Roger Goffe 1981

ISBN: 0 09 927200 8

Printed in Great Britain by The Guernsey Press Co Ltd,
Guernsey, Channel Islands.

IT'S KIDSTUFF

I didn't break
the saucer!

I just made
a jigsaw out
of it!

I AM FOUR.
SOON I'LL
BE FIVE
AND I'LL BE
WORSE THEN!

Dad, if you sort of swallow a ladybird, is it very serious?

Daddy always lets me play with his camera, but only when he's not there!

God, As my tortoise has died, will it be alright if I keep the shell and you send me a refill? Thank you God!

Mum, why are there so many fools on the road when you're driving?

I saw a kind
farmer taking
a whole lorry
load of sheep
for a nice
drive into town!

I only stroke dogs on the tail. They dont bite that end!

Mum's Ill so I have to be noisy Quietly!

Dads not Rich,

He's British!

My baby brother
was born just
after mum
finished being
pregnant!

I think I
Must love you
mum because
I don't come
home for the
pleasure!

I didn't have a
dream last night

I fell asleep
and missed it!

When you get married you go in a big car with lots of flowers on top!

Mum, shall I put the sweets on the top shelf, where I can't reach them?

Grannies are nice
old ladies who
stop Dads from
smacking you!

I got sunburnt and all my skin came undone!

My hobby is practising my autograph for when I'm famous!

Swimming with goggles isn't much fun, all you ever see is feet and bottoms!

if you're pregnant
and then get
a divorce, does
the bump go
down?

Only grownup
girls wear bra's
because its not
until then that
they go out of
shape!

You can tell when people are old because they wobble!

If I'm late for school a lot, will I get the sack?

Why dont they put sardines in jars so they can see out?

Mum, I stuck
your stamps
on the
shopping list
so they won't
blow away!

My dad's
a vicar. He
goes to church
and shouts
at people!

My Mums
cooking gives
me happy
memories
in my
tummy!

I didn't
hit her!
She grazed
herself
on me!

I always say out loud what I'm going to eat, so my stomach knows what to expect next!

Vicars dont laugh much because Jesus didnt tell any jokes!

I wasn't born
in the hospital,
I was born in
the house.
It's called being
home made!

Mum and Dad make me share everything with my sister!

I've just shared my measles!

Somebody is
always leaving
my room
on the floor!

Eyebrows are
for keeping
the shampoo
out of your
eyes!

I go to bed
every night!

why can't I
have a
night off?

I didn't say
"No thank you"
at the party,
because there
wasn't anything
I didn't want!

This left is
called **Left**
and the other
left is called
Right!

Why does Dad always put a teabag in his drink when he always throws it away?

Grandad
hides his
big cup
under the
bed!

When the vicar
christened my
brother he had
to wash his
face before he
could tell who
he was!

I put a whole
five pence in the
harvest festival
box but I still
didn't get a marrow!

Mum has a
new red blouse!
She looks lovely
just like a
lollipop!

Why have all my clothes had other people in them?

How can I
have chicken
pox when
we don't
even have
chickens?

I have a
tummy ache
Can I have
a plaster
for it?

Why do
cats only
sing at night?

I like to fetch
things from
downstairs
when something
good is on
telly!

My Mum doesn't
watch much T.V.
She likes
        watching
books instead!

I wish Mum would have twins, but she can't 'cos she only has one husband!

Why smack me?
I only hit her
to make sure
she'd like me!

I cooked my very first meal today. I've cooked toast on toast!

This morning I painted my toenails, and now I cant get my socks off!

This wall has shrunk!
it used to come up
to my chin, but
now it only comes
up to my tummy!

I keep
tripping up
because I've
cross eyed
feet!

My dads always putting money in parking meters but he never wins anything!

Every day I do a
drawing for teacher
she keeps them
safe in a big basket
under her desk!

I didn't cry! My eyes just dribbled!

I like Haggis, except for eating.

I'm so clever now,
I can get my
sums wrong the
first time!

Doesn't ANYONE make a clock without bedtime on it?

I have to love her even when I hate her 'cos she's my sister!

Teacher keeps
her mouth shut
at dinner time
So her chips
wont fall out!

Now my sister has her own baby, she's nasty to me in a nicer sort of way.

My dogs silly!
Every time I
Point something
out to him he
just looks at
my finger!

When Granny is in bed, she leaves her smile in a glass!

Teachers
Know more
than
grannies
or
humans!

Dad, how
much petrol
does it
take to
get to
heaven?

Worms can't fly, so why do birds sit in trees?

I liked my farm holiday. except for the smelly weather!

The wedding was lovely, and after, we all went to a great big conception party in a tent!

I didn't put a stamp on your letter Mum. I posted it when no one was looking!

Why don't baths
have doors so
I can get in
by myself!

What a lot of cards!
How did the
postman know it
was my birthday?

WHY, WHEN MUMS COLD DOES SHE TELL ME TO PUT A JUMPER ON?

Now I know
First Aid I
never, ever
fall over!
why?

A daughter
is a
lady son!

Cabbage
is my
worst
enemy!

We know our Mum isn't really having another baby because we only have four chairs!

I didn't have glue, so I stuck my boot with marmalade!

Whenever I play the piano, why does the music always get mixed up inside?

You have to get
your sums wrong
sometimes to
stop teacher
getting bored!

Why does the injection doctor always say "This wont hurt" when it's already hurting?

I hate my
reading book!
It has too many
words in it!

Mum said, she wants some toilet water for her birthday. Yuk!

If you eat red berries, you wake up dead!

Sometimes I help mummy work! I stay out of the way!

I like
plasticine
and puddings,
because they're
quiet and
peaceful.

Mum, if all that
stuff on your
face is to make
you more
beautiful, when
does it start
to work?

School dinner
was so revolting
today, I could
hardly eat my
second helping!

Why do pigs snore when theyre awake?

A prairie is a place where the cowboys go to play!

Mum, can I have some jogging shoes that dont have bad breath?

The worst part of
going to the dentist
Is all the crying
you have to do
afterwards!

When my sister grows up does that mean I'll have two mums?